# ten Dollars
### and a Rope

# Ten Dollars and a Rope

## Lois Salmonson

Xulon Press

Xulon Press
2301 Lucien Way #415
Maitland, FL 32751
407.339.4217
www.xulonpress.com

© 2019 by Lois Salmonson

All rights reserved solely by the author. The author guarantees all contents are original and do not infringe upon the legal rights of any other person or work. No part of this book may be reproduced in any form without the permission of the author. The views expressed in this book are not necessarily those of the publisher.

Unless otherwise indicated, Scripture quotations taken from the King James Version (KJV) – *public domain.*

Printed in the United States of America.

ISBN-13: 978-1-5456-7402-4

Dedicated to
My Daddy

*James William Davis*

January 12, 1925 – May 17, 2016

Thank you for keeping the Faith

# Acknowledgements

For my husband Johnny, my Kids, John, Jimmy and Jenny
*For loving me unconditionally*

For my brother Lynn,
*Who was always by my side when we were growing up. Thanks for being my friend and for being with me when we bought Cricket.*

For my siblings, Jimmy, Dorothy, Lynn, and Tommy
*Who had to put up with me and for the all the remember when's at our get togethers.*

For all my friends and family
*who encouraged me to write this book and for believing in me.*
I love all Ya.ll!

# Ten Dollars and a Rope

I GREW UP IN A SMALL TOWN CALLED ANNAVILLE, on a small road called Starlite Lane. It was the perfect place to grow up. Somebody even wrote a cute poem about it: "Star Light, star bright, first star I see tonight; I wish I may, I wish I might, have this wish I wish tonight." Of course, we all know that poem wasn't about the road I grew up on, but I was a kid, so I could believe whatever I wanted to. I would run out in the yard every evening just to wish on a star, and I made the same wish every time. My wish was: "I wish I had a horse." This little neighborhood was the perfect place to have a horse. Annaville was out in the country where people had room for horses, goats, chickens, and whatever farm animals they wanted.

We lived on half an acre. Now, that doesn't seem like a lot of land, but when you're a kid, it seems huge. It was a small community where everybody knew everybody, so we had the fun of roaming all over that little piece of the world. My daddy grew a sweet little garden every year, and we had most of our half-acre fenced off for our goats. We were poor and the only kind of animals we had were those for food, or that would provide milk, or whatever it took to feed our family. There were five of us kids in the family, living in a tiny little house filled with lots of love but not a lot of food or money.

Daddy did, however, always seem to have enough money to buy beer or to go to the bar, which I didn't understand. He liked playing pool, and he always went to this one little bar that he liked.

I guess when you want something bad enough, you rationalize for it. Mama didn't want him to be there without her, so they would pile all of us kids in the car, and off we would go. The five of us kids would sit in the car all night while Daddy played pool and had his beer. It wasn't such a bad thing back in the day for the kids to stay in the car while the parents went inside, at least they didn't leave us at home alone. Mama hated those nights, but she loved Daddy so much. She would sit in the car with us for a while, praying for Daddy before she went inside to be with him.

Mama grew up in a Christian home and went to church most of her life, so she started taking us to church when we were all pretty young. Daddy was not a Christian, and for a long time, he would just take us to church and come back afterward to take us back home. Then he started staying at church but remaining in the car and napping until the service ended. Pastor Davis would always go out to the car and invite Daddy to church, but Daddy always said no.

On one particular Sunday, Pastor Davis was standing by the car talking to Daddy, and it started raining Pastor Davis told Daddy he was going to stand there in the rain until Daddy agreed to go to church. Daddy told him he was such a bad person if he went in, the roof would cave in on everybody. Pastor Davis laughed and told Daddy roofs can be rebuilt, so Daddy promised to go in the next Sunday. Daddy was always true to his word. The next Sunday when Daddy took us to church, he too came into the church. He went in, accepted Jesus, and from that day forward our way of living in that little house on Starlite Lane changed. He gave up a lot of his old ways of living and concentrated on loving God and following His word. He took us all to church every time those doors were open. It was a good, simple, but poor life. It's so refreshing to watch a new Christian learn about God's love and faith.

So, anyway, back to my horse story. Knowing that a horse couldn't provide for us like other farm animals meant having one was a luxury, and we couldn't afford that kind of animal. But, knowing and accepting are two different things. I had asked Daddy several times for a horse, but he never would give in to the idea. It would cost too much money to own a horse; they eat a lot, and we just didn't have the money to feed one. Daddy would say things like, he didn't have two nickels to rub together, or if it cost a nickel to travel around the world, we couldn't even get to the end of the road. Who says that kind of stuff? I didn't know what most of that really meant, but I was smart enough to figure out his answer was just no, plain and simple. Saying no would have been easier for me to understand sometimes. I kind of knew we couldn't afford a horse, but adult logic just didn't make much sense to me. I was about ten years old and smart enough to understand no means no, but to throw in the nickels rubbing together thing just baffled me. Daddy worked long and hard to provide for us, but sometimes we had very little to eat. Being a little kid, I don't think I understood the value of money, nor did I care. I was just a kid, and my life was simple, and I was selfish and self-centered, *and* I just wanted a horse. It filled my every waking moment and even my dreams. It seemed like that was all my life was about, having my own horse.

    We were lucky enough to have a rodeo arena right behind our house, which was heaven on earth for me. Since I couldn't have a horse, the next best thing was hanging out at the horse barns at Scotts Rodeo Arena. I spent as much time as I could hanging out there—feeding horses, brushing horses, and chasing after baby ducks every now and then.

Of course, the ducks weren't the reason I was there; it was the horses. The dirtier I got and the more I smelled like the horses, the happier I was. One summer, Mr. Scott decided He wanted to have a Shetland pony auction. Oh my goodness, you can only imagine the joy in my heart. Just like in the cartoons I had this light bulb flashing over my head, bright as day I might add, and I was sure everybody could see what I was thinking: here was my chance to finally buy a horse. Now I know that Shetland ponies aren't "real" horses, at least that's what some people thought and what some people had the nerve to tell me. My thought was since they weren't as big as "real" horses, then they shouldn't cost as much as a "real" horse. They looked like a horse, and they smelled like a horse, so it was a horse. I knew I would be happy to have one.

The big day of the auction finally came around, and I was so excited. Mama knew my passion for a horse and knew I would be going over to the arena. Actually, any time she couldn't find me around the house, she would know I was probably over at the arena or horse barns. So, my going over there that day was surely no surprise to her. She worked long and hard hours also as a waitress at a local café. I would have asked her for some money if she had been home, but she couldn't get off work that day.

As it was time for me to head over, I found me a rope and a little bit of courage—or really a lot of courage—and walked up to Daddy to ask, "Can I have some money? I'm going over to that pony auction at Scotts Arena, and I'm going to buy me a horse."

Daddy just looked at me, and his expression didn't change much as he reached for his billfold. I would love to know what he was thinking, or maybe it was a good thing that I couldn't know what he was thinking. I was totally prepared for him to tell me no or give me some story about rubbing two nickels together or just to show me an empty billfold. Instead, he looked me square in the eye as he opened his billfold to show me what he had. Then, he handed me the ten-dollar bill that was there. Now his billfold was empty as he looked at me without saying a word and shrugged his shoulders. I didn't know what that meant, but I didn't want to stay around for long to find out either.

He just gave me all he had in his billfold, and I didn't know it at the time, but it was his last dollar. I didn't even think about the hardship it might put on my family. I didn't think about all the food it could have bought or bills it might have paid. All I knew was Daddy, who never gave money to us kids, had just handed me a ton of money. I felt like it could have been a million bucks, and I could buy anything I ever wanted with it. I was nervous, excited, and scared all at the same time. I was scared he would take the money back and then all chances of buying a horse would be gone. I didn't know it right then, but Daddy told me many years later that he had given me his last dollar because he knew he would be getting it back. No matter what I thought I would be able to buy with ten dollars, he knew I wouldn't be buying a horse with it.

## Ten Dollars and a Rope

Well, as we learned much later, God has plans we don't even know about. Daddy was a new Christian so what took place was a shock, or maybe some might say a miracle.

Oblivious to the world and walking on cloud nine, I walked out of the driveway with my brother, carrying a rope in my hands and Daddy's ten dollars. My brother and I were pretty close when we were growing up, so of course, he went with me to the auction. We found a seat on the bleachers, and boy, let me tell you, there were a lot of people there. I had never been to an auction before, so I didn't know what to expect. But, I assumed it couldn't be too hard to figure out. I was so wrong. The auction began with a crazy man speaking in a language I had never heard in my life. People were acting like they knew what was going on, and every now and then, they would raise their hand then look around all smug, acting like they just won some kind of major race or something. I felt out of place and had my first thought of not getting a horse. There was a knot in my stomach, and I thought I was going to be sick. This sure was a day for a roller coaster of emotions. I was so glad my brother was with me. He was the only one who really knew what I was feeling.

The ponies weren't selling as well as the owner thought they should, so he cancelled the auction. My heart sank even further, *how was I supposed to buy my horse now?* The owner decided to just tie the ponies up around the inside of the arena and let people go around to pick out which one they wanted to buy.

*Oh, thank goodness,* I thought, *I still have a chance.* The people swarmed the arena, picking out their ponies, paying for them, and leaving. My brother and I found this one tiny little pony and thought, since she wasn't as big as the others, she couldn't cost as much. We positioned ourselves between her and anybody who wanted to look at her, and we told them she was sold, she was ours. The owner was making his rounds and finally got to where we were standing with our horse. I held out my money and said, "I'm buying this pony; here's my ten dollars." He laughed at me and told me the pony was two hundred dollars and I should move out of the way so people with money could see her and buy her.

*Two hundred dollars!* My goodness, I had never seen that much money in my life, but I was smart enough to know there's a big difference between ten dollars and two hundred dollars. I felt hopeless and desperate. That sick feeling came back again but only for about two seconds. I had never been defiant with adults, but this time I held my ground. I repeated I was going to buy that pony and tried to give him my ten dollars again. He stopped in his tracks, turned around, gave me the meanest look, and then turned and walked away. Well, he sure didn't know me very well, and I hope he never forgot me either. Though none of us knew, God's plan was falling into place during this time.

People were still walking around the arena and would stop to look at our horse. My brother and I would keep maneuvering our way between them and the pony, telling them over and over again that she was sold. Every time the owner walked by, he would give me the evil eye. Still I would look back at him with the bravest look I could get on my face and hold out my ten dollars. I've never been so ignored in my whole life, but I was starting to get on his nerves. My mama finally showed up and, bless her heart, she gave me eighteen dollars then left. In my mind, she should have stayed around to give the "Mean Man" a piece of her mind. *Come on Mama, help me out a little,* but she didn't stay; she left me to fight this battle on my own. I wonder what was going on in her mind, thinking that me, a little ten-year-old girl, could handle this by myself. She didn't know I was face-to-face with a giant of a man with a mean face, and I suspected he didn't care much for little kids, and especially not for me. I did kind of feel bad that she had given me her eighteen dollars because I knew she had worked hard for it. At the same time, I felt richer than rich. I had never had so much money in my hands at one time. Her eighteen dollars and Daddy's ten dollars now made twenty-eight dollars, and I knew, without a doubt, that I could buy a horse now. MR. "Mean Man" wouldn't ignore me now.

Now, as a parent, when my kids want something, I do everything in my power to get it for them and to make them happy, and I think that's what my mama was doing. She probably knew it wouldn't help much, but she knew it would give me a little bit of hope. She didn't know Daddy had given me ten dollars, but seriously, how did she think I could buy a horse for eighteen dollars? Maybe she gave it to me with the same idea that Daddy had, that she would be getting her eighteen dollars back.

Mr. "Mean Man" was coming by again, so I stepped right in front of him and held up my money. I said, "I have twenty-eight dollars, and I'm buying this pony."

He reminded me of the price, as if I didn't know, then stepped around me, trying his best to ignore me—again. My patience was growing thin with this man, but I tried not to show it. My friend Mr. Scott, the owner of the arena, had been walking the rounds with Mr. "Mean Man" and keeping an eye on me and my dealings with him. I liked Mr. Scott a lot and didn't want him mad at me for being in the way at the pony sale. If he got mad at me, he might not let me hang around the horse barn and arena anymore.

At this point, I noticed Mr. Scott kind of hanging around the area where my brother and I were. I watched as he would talk with first one and then another of his cowboy friends, then he would look at us, and then his cowboy friends would look at us.

So now I was wondering just what was going on and how long it was going to take until he came over and asked me to please leave. I sure didn't want to leave, but I would if he asked me to. You can imagine how uncomfortable a little kid would be feeling, watching his or her friend hanging around with his cowboy friends and keeping an eye on you. He kept moving closer and closer to us, and I got a little more scared assuming I was just minutes away from being sent home. Just when I wasn't expecting it, Mr. Scott and I locked eyes, and he winked at me. My heart fluttered because I didn't know what to do or what was going on. That didn't look like a mean or mad face to me.

Again, Mr. "Mean Man" was making one of his rounds, and my heart began beating faster and faster. Despair and hope, despair and hope. How much more could I take? Mr. "Mean Man" was almost where my brother and I were standing when Mr. Scott stepped in front of him, talking and pointing to us. After their conversation, Mr. "Mean Man" came over to my brother and me and said, "Take the pony and get out of here," then he grabbed the money out of my hand. He was not very nice.

Mr. Scott, being a nicer man, came over and said, "Put your rope on the pony, honey. You can take her home now; she's yours."

I get choked up every time I think about that moment in my life. Those men never knew the huge impact they had on my Daddy's life that day. They didn't know they had just influenced a new Christian to believe and have faith that would last a lifetime and influence the way he lived from that day onward. To me, that day was a miracle; things like that don't just happen. I will always love Mr. Scott and his cowboy friends for their kind hearts. What we had just witnessed was unbelievable. The tiniest little pony you've ever seen was ours. Like I said though, she looked like a horse and smelled like a horse, so I was in heaven. We put the rope on her neck and walked her home.

When we got to the driveway, Daddy was still standing around in the yard. It seemed like we had been gone forever, but I don't really know how long it had been. It was unlike Daddy to hang around in the yard for hours, so I was confused. Maybe he was walking around the yard, thinking about me bringing home his ten dollars. He turned around and saw us coming up into the yard, and you should have seen the look on his face. Was this an *oh dear, how am I going to feed this horse?* look, or was it an *oh dear, how am I going to feed my family?* look? Then, wonder of wonders, he started smiling, and then his smile turned into a laugh.

I walked the little horse right up to Daddy and said, "I got a horse, but she ain't very big."

Daddy said since she was about as big as a cricket then that should be her name. Cricket. "Welcome home, Cricket." Daddy looked at me, shook his head, and said, "If that don't beat all—ten dollars and a rope. That's faith right there. If that don't beat all."

God used that day to show my daddy faith is one of the most important things in life. God doesn't always give us what we want, but sometimes He does. He just needs us to love Him and trust Him. I sure didn't need that horse, but Daddy, being a new Christian, needed to see how faith works and that God will provide for our needs.

A few years ago, Daddy told me it had indeed been his last dollar, but when he saw me standing there with a rope in my hand, he just didn't have the heart to tell me no. That and he knew he would be getting his money back. So, he wasn't really worried. He didn't know I fully intended on bringing home a horse; why else would I be taking a rope? But, I didn't see it as faith. I just wanted a horse. I was a small child on a mission.

Daddy grew to have an immense love for God and faith like I've never seen in anybody else in my life. The funny thing is he always felt like he never had enough faith. He told me he always felt like those people in the Bible who roamed around the desert for so long because of their lack of faith. Psalm 91:1 talks about those who dwell in the secret place of the Most High shall abide under the shadow of the Almighty. Daddy said he didn't feel worthy of dwelling in the secret place and that he always walked on the edge of the shadow because of his lack of faith. Trust me when I tell you, my daddy walked in the shadow of the almighty. If Daddy didn't have enough faith, then I don't have a chance. He learned that God provides for us just like He provided for His children in the desert. It was all just a good lesson for both of us. We saw that if we depend on God, He will take care of us. I grew up with a daddy who would always put God first, no matter what. Every time I would go visit Daddy we would talk about ten dollars and a rope. We would laugh and thank God for loving us so much and for all our blessings.

Our little horse lived a long, well-fed, and happy life. Out of five kids, not a single one of us went without food either. God provided. Isn't He good? Ten dollars and a rope. If that don't beat all. Who would have thought it?

Hebrews 11:1 - "Faith is the assurance of things hoped for the conviction of things not seen."

Matthew 17:20 - "If you have faith like a grain of mustard seed, nothing will be impossible."

CPSIA information can be obtained
at www.ICGtesting.com
Printed in the USA
LVIC060044291019
635652LV00004B/205